HUNTING LABS

WILLOW CREEK PRESS

Minocqua, Wisconsin

HUNTING LABS

Photography by
DENVER BRYAN

Text by
E. DONNALL THOMAS JR.

WILLOW CREEK PRESS
Minocqua, Wisconsin

Dedication

Every bird hunter who has ever been fortunate enough to share even a few years with a Labrador retriever
during their lifetime knows what a good hunting dog brings to one's days afield. Memories of a retriever chasing
a wounded duck repeatedly diving below the surface of the marsh to avoid being apprehended, but to no avail;
a broken-wing, but very-much-alive pheasant in the mouth of your dog that disappeared on its trail 10 minutes earlier;
the look in your dog's eyes after you've missed a half dozen shots in a row. "Wonderful are the days spent traipsing afield
for both waterfowl and upland birds, but more wonderous are those days shared with a good dog."

It has been my good fortune to have spent countless days afield photographing and hunting with numerous Lab owners
over the past several years. I owe the following no small debt of gratitude for putting up with my constantly-probing cameras:
Marc and Bridger Pierce, Jared and Greg Brown, Kern Stevenson, Mike Atwell, Jason Wise, Dave Cocoran,
Heather Andrews, Nate Jorgenson, Eric Pierce, Ray Basta, Jobie Sabol, Jeff Lawrence, Larry McMurry, John Bouchert,
Dana Giovanello, Brad McMurtrey, E. Donnall Thomas, Dennis Potzman, Tony Schoonen, Peyton Randolph,
Pete and Tanya Rothing, Pat Harlin and Patrick Moran.

And as always, the dogs that enrich the whole hunting experience...

Denver Bryan

Text © 2003 E. Donnall Thomas Jr.
Photography © 2003 Denver Bryan

Editor: Andrea Donner
Design: Katrin Wooley

Published by Willow Creek Press
P.O. Box 147, Minocqua, Wisconsin 54548
www.willowcreekpress.com

Library of Congress Cataloging-in-Publication Data
Bryan, Denver.
    Hunting Labs : a breed above the rest / photography by Denver Bryan ;
text by E. Donnall Thomas.
      p. cm.
    ISBN 1-57223-703-1 (alk paper)
    1. Labrador retriever.   2. Labrador retriever--Pictorail works.   3. Hunting dogs.
    4. Hunting dogs--Pictorail works.   I. Thomas, E. Donnall.   II. Title.
      SF429.L3B77 2003
      636.752'7--dc21
                                                            2003008862

Printed in South Korea

Table of Contents

A BRIEF HISTORY OF LABS
You can't know the dogs without knowing their background

They flush pheasants and fetch ducks, guide the blind and sniff out contraband at border crossings, lick faces and enrich lives. At some point, every Lab enthusiast must wonder about the origins of the remarkable animal that has become the most popular dog in America. In fact, the Lab's history turns out to be laced with enough intrigue to fuel a spy novel, reflecting the difficulties of reconstructing events that took place over three centuries, across one ocean and in two nations divided, as one sage noted, by a common language.

Archimedes observed that given a fulcrum he could move the world. In similar fashion, unraveling historical mysteries often goes best by starting with an event generally accepted as true, even if that means beginning in the middle of the story. The British Col. Peter Hawker probably provided the first written description of the Lab in his 1814 treatise *Instructions to Young Sportsmen*. Referring to the St. John's dog in distinction from the larger, more familiar Newfoundland, he wrote: "The other, by far the best for every kind of shooting, is oftener black than of another color, and scarcely

bigger than a pointer. He is made rather long in the head and nose; pretty deep in the chest; very fine in the legs; has short or smooth hair; does not carry his tail so much curled as the other; and is extremely active in running, swimming..." All of which sounds pretty much like someone we know.

While it's relatively easy to follow the trail forward from the British St. John's dog of the early 19th century to the modern Lab, tracing the Lab's ancestry from the coast of Newfoundland to Hawker's day proves far more involved. Writers, alas, must bear their share of responsibility for the confusion. When the Lab returned to the New World as a popular East Coast sporting breed in the 1900s, commentators created a history to accompany it. In the process, they perpetuated two central ideas: that the Lab derived from the Newfoundland and that the Newfoundland in turn derived from indigenous New World

canines. Unfortunately, both ideas are probably untrue.

Abundant evidence confirms that Native Americans lived and hunted with large dogs. But British explorers reached the coast of Newfoundland as early as 1494, and there is no reliable record of dogs in the area until British fishermen arrived two centuries later. The romantic notion that our Labs' genes originated here in North America enjoys little objective support. On the contrary, the breed's ancestors almost certainly crossed the Atlantic as working dogs employed by Devon fishermen plying their dangerous trade

along Newfoundland's rugged coast.

As for the derivation of the Lab (then known as the St. John's dog) from the Newfoundland, the late Richard Wolters has done a brilliant job of proving it was probably the other way around. In the face of sketchy direct evidence, Wolters argued that the dog's original job description favored the smaller breed, which had to crowd into cramped dories while waiting for a chance to fetch lines, nets, and fish for its masters. The appearance of the larger Newfoundland coincided with the later development of permanent settlements along the coast, when colonists needed large, powerful dogs to haul heavy loads of firewood.

And what were the origins of the dog that crossed the Atlantic to the New World in the first place?

The most likely candidate for the title of Lab's Ultimate Ancestor is the St. Hubert's hound, originally of French origin but plainly popular in England at the time Newfoundland's first settlers embarked. Definitive answers remain elusive, but both the written descriptions and drawings of this breed in George Turbervile's *Booke of Hunting*, published in 1576, bear a striking resemblance to modern Labs.

By this complex route, the St. John's dog became a popular British sporting breed in the early 1800s, as evidenced by Delabere Blaine's description of the breed in his *Encyclopedia of Rural Sports*, published in 1840. "The St. John's breed is preferred by sportsmen on every account, being smaller, more easily managed and sagacious in the extreme. His scenting powers are also great... Gentlemen have found them so intelligent, so faithful, and so capable of general instruction that they have given

up most sporting varieties and content themselves with these..." And along the way the breed acquired its enduring name when the popular sporting artist Edward Landseer painted *Cora: A Labrador Bitch*, in 1823.

Unfortunately, the Lab's reputation fared better during the 19th century than the dogs themselves. American independence and changes in the fishing trade decreased direct commerce between the breed's point of origin in Newfoundland and the new market for them among the British aristocracy. Attempts to promote a sheep industry in Newfoundland

No matter how highly English sportsmen valued Labs, a shortage of breeding stock threatened the breed with extinction.

led to new restrictions on dog rearing there. No matter how highly English sportsmen suddenly valued Labs, they couldn't get enough of them to maintain breeding stock and the breed faced the serious threat of extinction.

But there are no friends like friends in high places, and the Lab was fortunate enough to enjoy the favor of just the right people. During the first half of the 19th century, the 2nd Lord of Malmesbury, the 5th Duke of Buccleuch, and the 10th Earl of Home, all avid sportsmen and Lab enthusiasts, established breeding programs and went to considerable lengths to import what fresh breeding stock they could from Newfoundland. All fortunately had children interested in maintaining the family kennels, and while none seemed particularly interested in sharing their blood lines with anyone but each other, they managed to preserve the Lab during the most precarious period

in the dogs' history.

While all modern Labs derive from limited bloodlines developed and maintained by a few aristocratic families, by the beginning of the 20th century Labs had truly started to thrive in England and Scotland. The British Kennel Club officially recognized the breed as distinct in 1903. Labs began

attracting serious attention in field trials and bench shows, and Viscount Knutsford and Lorna Countess Howe established the Labrador Club in 1916. Back from the brink in England, it was time for the breed to realize the next formative step in its development, which it did by crossing the Atlantic once again.

Charles Meyer registered the first Labrador retriever with the American Kennel Club in 1917. Because American wingshooters of the day approached the field so differently than their staid British counterparts, they viewed their sporting dogs differently as well. They taught their pointers and setters to retrieve as a matter of course, leaving no defined job description for the pure retriever in the pursuit of upland game. Chesapeake Bay retrievers handled the serious work in the water. The Rodney Dangerfields of the sporting world, retrievers didn't enjoy a lot of respect. As late as 1927 there were fewer than thirty retrievers registered with the AKC, all — Labs, Chessies, Goldens, Flat Coated and Curly Coated — lumped together under the single category of "Retriever."

In characteristic fashion, the amiable Lab — backed by a new

generation of enthusiastic American admirers — set about changing all that. Initially, the Lab's reputation as a favorite of the British aristocracy helped fuel the breed's popularity among America's status conscious *nouveau riche*, the social class to which most early Lab importers belonged. But it was only a matter of time until the breed's reputation began to dissem-inate to the general sporting public, largely as the result of the dogs' performance in field trials. The new American Labrador Retriever Club held the breed's first trial in 1931. Although the tests were hardly demanding by today's standards, the event drew considerable attention. By the end of the decade, Lab trials had become popular, well-publicized events attended by amateur handlers as well as the professionals who originally managed dogs for their wealthy owners.

The history of the Lab's development as a field trial star during the middle of the last century is well documented. Meanwhile, to considerably less fanfare, other events were taking place that in my opinion contributed just as much to the breed's eventual development into the Lab we know today. Introduced to Oregon in the 1880s (as described in Chapter Three), the ringneck pheasant expanded its range across the Midwest, attracting a major following among everyday American sportsmen in the process. In contrast to the quail, woodcock and grouse that defined the upland gun dog's original American job description, pheasants favored heavy cover, ran relentlessly before flushing, and proved exceptionally difficult to recover after the shot. The explosion of interest in outdoor sports that followed the end of the Second World War found American upland hunters in sore need of a new type of gun dog that could beat the wily ringneck at its own game. The demands of pheasant hunting practically defined the previously unknown concept of the flushing retriever, and the Lab proved ideally suited to fill this complex new job description.

And as Labs replaced Chessies in the duck blind and pointers in the field, a subtle change took place in the everyday relationship between the dogs and their owners. In 19th century Britain and even during the early years of the Lab's introduction to America, sporting dogs largely existed to entertain the rich. Cared for by servants and trained by professional handlers, Labs of that era enjoyed a distant, largely impersonal relationship with those who owned them and determined the future of the breed. But as Labs

The Lab proved ideally suited to fill a complex new job description: flushing retriever.

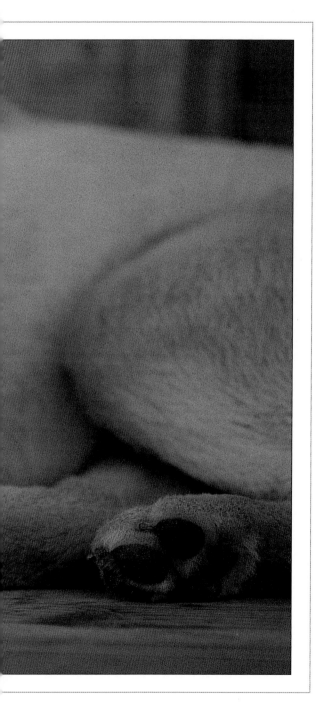

grew more versatile in the field, they became popular among Americans of all walks of life. Rather than retiring automatically to the kennel at the end of the day, they rode around in trucks, lounged in front of fireplaces, and played with kids. In short, they became family dogs, and the personality traits that suited their new role in life became as highly regarded as the courage and tenacity that had made them popular in the field.

It doesn't take a genius to recognize my residence as a Lab haven. As I finish this piece, Sonny — the Grand Old Man — lies upstairs on his favorite corner of the dining room rug taking a nap, which is what he does best these days. Jake is circling the house looking for the sharptails that drop in from time to time over the winter. The birds aren't around today, but he doesn't seem to care. And Rocky is picking through a box full of fly-tying materials looking for something that tastes like a bird. Each in his own way, they're all being Labs, and knowing where they came from helps me appreciate them just a little bit more.

 _____

As Labs grew more versatile in the field, their popularity as pets grew also. Rather than retire to the kennel at the end of the day, they lounged in front of the fireplace or played with the kids.

LADIES AND GENTLEMEN
Viva la difference

I grew up in a family that viewed the outdoors as an equal opportunity resource without regard to gender, and over the years I've enjoyed the company of my mother, sister, wife, and daughters in the field. Nonetheless, I admit I've spent a lot more time working with male Labs than their female counterparts. Some of that discrepancy derives from chance, since the two best Labs I've ever raised happened to be males and like all Lab enthusiasts, I've tried to reproduce what's worked well for me in the past. But I've spent my share of time around females of the breed as well, and what I've learned from both sexes has defied established gender stereotypes nearly as often as it's enforced them.

Classical books on dog training tended to present behavioral differences between male and female canines as if they were cast in stone, a reflection, no doubt, of prevailing social attitudes that treated distinctions between men and women much the same way. According to traditional theory, Lab handlers could expect females to be tractable, reasonable and sensitive, males to be aggressive, strong-willed and defiant. Prospective owners were encouraged to choose the gender of their puppies according to this simple Dogs-are-from-Mars, Bitches-are-from-Venus formula. But while there's certainly some validity to these ideas, like all generalizations, they often break down when applied to individuals. Furthermore, anyone who believes in them strongly enough runs the risk of creating a self-fulfilling prophecy.

While I've always done my best to treat my Labs in basically gen-der-neutral fashion, I can't deny that residual cultural attitudes have probably influenced my own approach to their upbringing, just as they've influenced the way I've raised my children. Giving males and females (of either species)

equal opportunities to realize their potential can't disguise the fact that, as the French have so famously noted, the sexes really are different. And so, some purely personal observations on those differences, including stereotypical expectations both realized and defied.

Around the house, male Labs often demonstrate what I characterize as aggressive affection... aggressive not so much in manner as in their refusal to be denied

human company. I spend a lot of my time indoors writing, and both Jake and Rocky practically insist on being involved in the process. It's not enough for them to wander into the study and flop down in a corner. Both dogs will sit beside me and stare at the computer screen as if they're checking my spelling. Distracting? I've grown so accustomed to their ways that I hardly notice. I suppose that when they start barking at my mistakes I'll have to credit them with a share of the byline.

Becca and Sherry — our last two female Labs — always seemed more diffident in similar situations. If the door to the study was open, they'd come and go, but they'd never sit outside and whine

until granted entrance. Maybe they were just willing to acknowledge that Labs can't really read. Then again, perhaps their tastes were just too sophisticated for my writing.

The territorial imperative probably illustrates fundamental differences between the canine sexes as obviously as any trait. Certainly anyone who has spent time observing male dogs being male dogs can appreciate the degree to which they take seriously both the definition and defense of their turf. And that territorial imperative doesn't stop at the door. Each of my three reigning males has established a *querencia*, to borrow a term from bullfight terminology: a spot on the floor chosen apparently at random to which the dog will inevitably retreat when scolded, tired, or just plain out of alternatives. Their predictability in these matters remains as mysterious as their reason for choosing their favorite spot in the first place.

Neither Becca nor Sherry, on the other hand, seemed to care much where they came to rest at the end of the day, as long as they weren't consigned to the indignity of the kennel. I finally reached the conclusion that they regarded the whole house as their spot, a global expression of nesting instinct that

let them bypass a lot of guy-thing silliness.

In the field, gender performance differences reflect trends rather than ironclad distinctions. I've certainly hunted with female Labs that demonstrated admirable tenacity and perseverance. And the fact that male dogs tend to win big field trials may simply reflect the fact that performance standards arbitrarily favor the way male dogs do things, an example of the self-fulfilling prophecy principle mentioned earlier.

But subject to the limits of generalization, I have noticed differences in the way male and female dogs approach their jobs in the field. Sherry, for example, was a strong performer in the water,

undaunted by challenging conditions and determined to stay focused. But in contrast to most of my males, she always left me with the impression that she considered fetching ducks a temporary amusement rather than an end unto itself. Workmanlike as she could be, she didn't scan the sky endlessly between sets of birds, and at the end of even the toughest retrieves, she'd curl up quickly at my feet as if she had more important things to think about than birds and praise and bonding. Whatever, as

my teenage daughters would say. While it's never safe to generalize based on observations of one dog, I've seen similar behavior from enough other females to consider this a valid observation. Perhaps the belief that nothing could possibly be more important than duck hunting remains another of those intangible guy-things. As much as she loves to hunt, I doubt Lori would disagree.

As if to emphasize the perils of stereotype, I've seen two traits ordinarily regarded as almost exclusively male reach their fullest expression in female Labs. Running off can be frustrating and time consuming for the owner and dangerous for the dog, and the usual reluctance of females to indulge in this aggravating behavior is frequently advanced as an argument for choosing one in the

first place. But I've never owned a Lab that liked to go AWOL with as much determination as Becca. What she was up to when she disappeared into the wild coulees surrounding our home remains a mystery and I'm sure I probably don't want to know. But she proved incorrigible, which is why she was one of the few Labs I've ever owned that didn't enjoy free run of the place.

As watchdogs, most Labs embody the principle of *all bark but no bite*. With a house full of Labs, no one is going to arrive at our house unannounced, and at least in his younger years, Sonny

was capable of putting on quite a show when an unfamiliar face appeared at the door. But anyone who understands dogs could see through his performances eventually, and a visitor willing to toss a few dummies could have enjoyed the run of the house within minutes of arrival. The willingness to

Subject to the limits of generalization, I have noticed differences in the way male and female dogs approach their jobs in the field.

befriend is an integral part of the Lab's personality, after all. That's one reason we have them around in the first place.

If anyone were to encounter real aggression from a Lab in such circumstances, most would expect it from a male. Those who operate on this blithe assumption should be forewarned before they meet an aging yellow female named Goldie. I gave Goldie to my parents as a pup only to have her turn into the only Labrador retriever I know that I've never been able to befriend. It isn't anything personal between the two of us. Goldie will put up her hackles and get right in the face of anyone who happens to come near my mother and father. And it's not just show, either. I've been around dogs long enough to recognize the bite beneath the bark, and Goldie means business. Her aggression troubled me at first, but since my folks are getting along in years and live in an urban environment where burglaries do

take place, I've come to terms with it. Anyone breaking into the senior Thomas residence can expect way more than they've bargained for, especially if they believe the conventional wisdom about female Labs and their mellow dispositions.

Conclusions? Gender defies stereotype, in Labs as well as people. Count on this much: females will require spaying or restraint when in season, males will wander when tempted. And consider this probable: female pups will mature into dogs that require less correction and restraint while their male counterparts will likely bond more strongly under adverse conditions. But *probable* allows plenty of room leeway, and no generalization should prevent a dog from reaching its potential in the home or the field.

Besides, they're all just Labs in the end.

MEETING IN THE HEARTLAND
How an Asian bird and a European dog came to define Autumn in America

The assault upon the senses begins at once: the riot of crimson and gold spilling across the hillside; the subtle scent of dry autumn foliage; the insistent chorus of migrating geese winging southward at high altitude. The air feels crisp against the skin despite the brilliance of the sun overhead, creating a momentary dissonance with the warmth of the autumn colors. The terrain ahead promises lots of up and down, but with weeks of hunting season already under our belts, the pitch of the coulees suggests challenges rather than obstacles.

Full of piss and vinegar, Sonny hops down from the truck with the focused attitude of a dog on a mission. I've always felt that he somehow regards hunting pheasants as different than everything else we do together in the field. He seemed to treat the sharptails and Huns we chased in September as practice, and even the teal we killed on the opening morning of duck season didn't seem to arouse anything more than a workmanlike determination to do what Labs are supposed to do. Today is different. He knows what lies ahead, and he's strutting around like a proud athlete eager to show the world his stuff.

Then again, perhaps I'm just projecting my own determination upon the dog. As much as I enjoy hunting sharptails and Huns, I've never really derived any sense of vindication from knocking them out of the sky, and for me duck blinds have always been about pageantry as much as killing. But pheasants are different. Their devious ways always seem personally directed, like trash talk on a basketball court or street corner disrespect. Whenever I hunt pheasants, the kid gloves come off. Today isn't about the beauty of the surroundings or the philosophical nature of the hunt. Today is about kicking butt.

The section of creek bottom we plan to hunt belongs to an old friend. I've had so much fun out here over the years that I'd feel guilty about it except that Lori and I have had the opportunity to help him and his family out a time or two in our day-job capacities as doctor and nurse. No one keeps

score; it isn't that kind of relationship. I'm just glad he's out here keeping an eye on the country and he's glad I'm in there (sometimes, at least) keeping an eye on him. The medical profession has had its problems over the last decade, but every time I drive through that gate, I'm glad I stuck with it all these years even when the urge to bail out and become a full-time outdoor literary bum felt all but overwhelming.

With the dog at heel and Lori carrying the camera, we cross the lip of the rise overlooking the creek and precipitate a remarkable explosion of sight and sound. The idea of counting pheasants proves instantly impossible. Clouds of birds are rising from the edge of the stubble and sailing away on locked wings toward the nastiest brambles imaginable. Bear in mind; it's early in the season, this cover has not been hunted, and we have done nothing but crest the horizon at a range ordinarily associated with hunting antelope with flat-shooting rifles. Our rig looks just like the pickup that drives by twice a day checking cows. But somehow the birds know, and the uncanny certainty of their knowledge explains why I want to kill three of them with three shots, watch three great retrieves, declare victory, and retire form the field before they can figure out a way to turn the tables.

"That is one hell of a lot of pheasants!" Lori observes and I have to agree. My activities so far this fall have all taken place far

Wild pheasants, rough terrain, and eager Labs define the old British concept of rough shooting.

from the pheasant cover and I really haven't had an opportunity to assess the year's hatch. In this regard, the sight of all those birds feels reassuring. But when Lori goes on to suggest that a three-bird limit ought to be easy, I must beg to differ. I know the cover the birds entered, just as I know what to expect from ringnecks in this kind of mood. Birds? Yes. Three of them? Possibly. Easy? I don't think so, not today, not on this planet.

Calling softly to the dog, I drop a pair of shells into the shotgun and set off to pick up the thrown gauntlet.

Beautiful, wily and delightful on the table, the ringneck pheasant has appealed to the human imagination since the dawn of recorded history. Three thousand year-old Chinese drawings depict the species in reverential tones. Marco Polo reported that the Kublai Khan maintained uncut fields of millet solely for the benefit of the royal pheasant population. And none of these enthusiasts even enjoyed the company of good dogs or the pleasure of fine guns.

The ringneck might have remained another Old World exot-

ic but for the enthusiasm of one Owen Denny, then the American consul to Shanghai. In 1881, intrigued by the bird's sporting potential, he shipped a crate of them to his brother's farm in Oregon's Willamette Valley where the new arrivals not only thrived but enjoyed an enthusiastic reception in their brave new world.

The next formative event in the pheasant's North America saga took place far away in Sarajevo, when an assassin's bullet felled Archduke Ferdinand and precipitated the War to End All Wars. At the time, Russia exported most of the world's wheat supply through strategically precarious Black Sea shipping lanes, which were promptly closed by Turkish blockade. Subsequent market pressures

spurred the development of dry land grain farming across the American Great Plains, and soon the ringneck enjoyed vast expanses of food-rich habitat. The rest, as they say, is history.

Meanwhile, American hunters were enjoying the benefits of more Old World genetics introduced from the opposite direction — Labrador retrievers originally derived from an obscure British dog known as St. Hubert's hound. The modern Lab's ancestors first reached American shores courtesy of the Devon fishermen who settled the coast of Newfoundland, where the dogs earned their keep fetching lines and nets from the icy waters of the North Atlantic. It took another roundtrip across the Big Pond and back for the breed to develop its sporting potential as a water retriever. By the time Denny's gift spread its way across the west, the Lab had become a favorite among waterfowlers along the eastern seaboard. Upland

work, however, remained the domain of the pointing breeds.

But as pheasant hunting increased in popularity, enthusiasts recognized the need for a new kind of bird dog. The arrivals from China didn't play by the same rules as ruffed grouse, woodcock, and quail. They could run *and* they could hide, employing thick cover to every advantage. The hunter's problem wasn't so much

finding them as getting them airborne within shotgun range. Eventually, the pheasant prompted the introduction of a new concept in sporting dogs: the flushing retriever.

And how uniquely suited to the spirit of the American frontier this development proved! Forget the decorum of European driven pheasant shoots and the elegance of bobwhite taken over braces of pointers. Wild pheasants, rough terrain, and eager Labs defined the old British concept of rough shooting and all its implications: legwork rather than leisure, thorns instead of tea and crumpets, the same irreverent triumph of the spirit that produced the American Revolution in the first place. The birds may have derived from Asia and the dogs from the British Isles, but their ultimate fusion belonged to us alone.

And I feel privileged to celebrate this happy confluence of events every chance I get.

Meanwhile, back at the ranch...

I was right about one thing: it hasn't been easy. Down in the willows and the beaver workings, the birds have led us on a merry chase. Sonny has done his job well enough, but every bird that has flushed in range managed to do so from behind an impenetrable screen of cover. The one rooster that offered something like a shot

left my swing aborted by a picket fence of brush. The sun has burned away the last of the chill as sweat rolls down my brow. Sonny wants a warm bird in his mouth just as badly as I want one in my hand, but he's too experienced to suggest complaint. This isn't frustration. It's pheasant hunting.

The thing to do now is to bear down, to believe the cover will produce what we want, and above

all not to get careless with the shooting when the first bird makes a potentially fatal mistake. All it takes is a little more time, a few more licks from the wild rose thorns, and continued resolve — we hope. Finally, Sonny puts his nose to the ground and begins to work his way toward an open bend in the little creek.

Surrounded by a loop of water, the birds have no place to go but up.

If it weren't for the dog, of course, all would be lost. I would

step right over the birds that choose to hide and chase the rest in a futile circle toward their eventual freedom. But Sonny and I have played this game before. Confirming Lori's position safely behind me, I stand and wait for him to work the cover, an occasion to which he rises with all the determination our long trip through the brambles can inspire.

It's hard to ignore a feeling of disappointment at the sight of the first rise. Drab and uninspiring, the bird is a hen, biologically critical to the species but not what we have come for today. But a rich cackle follows closely upon the sound of her wings and the gunstock is half way to my shoulder before the rooster appears in an eruption of noise and color. *Don't blow this*, I remind myself. *You owe one to the dog.*

The silence that follows the shotgun's report seems definitive, as if I have extinguished something larger than a bundle of wings and feathers. But the look on Sonny's face when he delivers the rooster to my outstretched hand erases any ambiguity I might feel about the kill. He knows we collected this bird the old fashioned way. We *earned* it.

"Ready for another easy one?" I ask Lori as she kneels to snap a few photos of Sonny and the bird.

"I don't know whether I've got another one in me," she admits. But I do, and so does Sonny.

Thanks, Mr. Denny. We needed that.

 _____

WHOSE BEST FRIEND?

No one really knows a dog like a duck hunter

With gray scud obscuring the landscape and horizontal rain driving against the windows of the tiny cabin, the October cold front made a persuasive argument for turning up the oil stove and crawling back inside my sleeping bag. But I wanted to go duck hunting and so did Sky. After all, that was the mission we'd flown across Cook Inlet the night before to accomplish. Using the security of the airplane as an excuse to venture outside, I climbed into my woolens and opened the door to the weather. Once I'd confirmed that the Cub had survived the night in its tie-downs, I returned to the cabin for my shotgun and a pack full of decoys, and then the dog and I set off together across the tide flats.

No place enforces the notion of solitude like wilderness Alaska, for reasons that go beyond the bear tracks and the weather. It's the delicious loneliness of the place that defines the mood, the realization that there's no one around to bother you — or to help you, for that matter — whether you want others there or not. Sharing a wilderness camp with bad company can be an excruciating experience, but sharing one with those you enjoy infuses the idea of friendship with new meaning. And good company can come from dogs as well as people.

In fact, I'm not sure I would have made it out of the sleeping bag that morning if it hadn't been for Sky. His incessant tail-wagging back in the cabin's dim interior reminded me how badly he wanted to hunt, and it's never easy to ignore that kind of enthusiasm. Fallen ducks in cold water can make a persuasive argument for hunting with a good retriever, but sometimes the dogs' real value lies in their ability to discourage the rest of us from taking the easy way out.

Because of the weather we didn't travel far that morning, but we

didn't have to. A short hike across the flats brought us to the edge of a little tidal basin where I tossed out a handful of decoys and huddled down in the dead grass next to the dog. The storm had brought waves of waterfowl down from the interior and little flocks of puddle ducks — green-wings, pintails, and mallards — dropped their landing gear and floated into our spread until I'd shot all I cared to shoot. I thought about braving the elements long enough to add a few geese to the bag, but the dampness seeping in around the edges of my rain gear convinced me it was time to declare victory and withdraw from the field. On the hike back to the security of the cabin, even Sky seemed comfortable with the decision.

By mutual agreement with my absent partners, we weren't supposed to let dogs into the hunting cabin and a row of airline kennels lined the porch to accommodate our canine friends. While I'd

already fudged on this rule the night before, there's a big difference between a clean, dry dog and a wet one covered with tidal mud after a morning of vigorous hunting. But Sky had served me too well to be consigned to a cold kennel. Out on the porch, I toweled him down with an old shirt and bid him enter while I prepared a breakfast of braised teal and canned beans appropriated from the store of staples we kept under the kitchen table. And as the heat from the oil stove filled the cabin with the smell of wet wool and wet dog, we sat down to one of the best hot meals imaginable — together.

Last year, the American Kennel Club accepted over 100,000 registration applications for Labrador retrievers, confirming the Lab's status as the country's most popular canine breed. Strange as it may seem to those of us who find retrievers and hunting inseparable,

many — if not most — of those dogs will never hear a shotgun's bark or gaze eagerly skyward as sets of wings cut the air overhead. And I'm not sure just what to make of this development.

Most of those dogs will enjoy happy lives in good homes and many will find service in a variety of capacities ranging from seeing-eye dog to backyard babysitter. But will they ever really enjoy the

opportunity to be Labs, and will their owners be able to say they know their charges? I'm skeptical. I recently had a non-hunting Lab owner ask me how anyone could make dogs jump into icy water to fetch a duck. Had she truly understood the breed, she might have asked how anyone could refuse to let them.

At least that's the way Sky and I always saw matters. In fact, neither of us would have had it any other way.

Another dog, another marsh, another season. The prairie's broad expanse has replaced the jagged peaks of the Alaska range. Instead of ominous, stormy weather, clear skies sprawl overhead and the evening air lies so still I can hear a chorus of redwings churring in the distance. But despite all the differences between the beginning of Montana's duck season and the end of Alaska's, some factors remain constant: the worn, familiar feel of

the shotgun in my hands, the oddly relaxed quality of our anticipation as we scan the horizon for birds, the easy feel of the companionship the dog and I have learned to share.

Up until an hour ago, I'd been enjoying a perfect example of a lousy day. The details aren't important. Everyone has a story to tell about life's inequities and I won't bore readers with mine. What matters is the delicious sense of escape I experienced as soon as I left work and headed out of town to try to salvage something from the last hour of shooting light, how quickly and completely I began to feel whole again instead of fractured. Best of all, I get to enjoy good company without having to listen to anyone complain in return.

Credit for this social miracle goes to West Wind's Sunrise, now age three. Like Sky before him, Sonny has his share of faults and we'll critique them honestly

No aspect of the working retriever's job description emphasizes the importance of canine personality like duck hunting.

enough when the time comes. But in addition to sharing many of Sky's attributes in the field (for better or worse), Sonny also demonstrates much of his predecessor's talent for making me glad he's there. No test measures this ability, which is hard enough to define let alone standardize. But, like art, you know it when you see it and sometimes that quality matters more than precise marking ability or perfect water entries.

No aspect of the working retriever's job description emphasizes the importance of canine personality like duck hunting. When upland birds aren't cooperating, hunters and dogs can simply pick up the pace until they find game. But waiting over decoys is usually a passive affair in which the birds are something that happens to you rather than the other way around. What you see is what you get and it's always nice to have company to share your fate whether it consists of waves of mallards or stubbornly vacant skies. I certainly spend a lot more time talking to my human friends when we're hunting ducks than I do when we're hunting

pheasants. Furthermore, upland hunting allows plenty of personal space, which offers an easy solution to the problem of dogs and handlers getting on each other's nerves. But it's hard to ignore a dog when you're sharing a duck blind. Such familiarity may not breed outright contempt, but close quarters always magnify the least likable traits of your company, human or otherwise.

Retrieving talents aside, it's hard to conceive of a dog breed better suited to close range companionship over long periods of time than the Labrador retriever. Despite my enthusiasm for Labs, I've enjoyed plenty of experience with other sporting dogs and find it difficult to imagine spending

hours on a hard bench in the rain beside a pointer or a hound. Like good dancers, Labs always seem willing to take cues from their partners, interacting when you want to hear from them and curling up unobtrusively when you don't. These welcome canine personality traits probably evolved by selection centuries ago when the modern Lab's ancestors spent long periods at sea with fishermen off the coast of Nova Scotia. Since an

open dory miles from shore may be even less conducive to the tolerance of bad company than a duck blind, personable dogs no doubt became breeding stock while troublemakers were invited to sleep with the fish — literally or figuratively.

The relationship that develops between dogs and hunters under demanding conditions in the field represents a reciprocal process. Despite the breed's growing popularity, I've always maintained that no one can ever understand a Lab as well as a hunter. Divorced from

their own background, Labs become reduced to pets. I've always found something depressing about that idea, which reminds me of watching a lion aimlessly pace its cage in a zoo. "Be all you can be," the army recruiting slogan urges, but a Lab destined to live out its years without watching a duck drop from the sky never will. Non-hunting friends who own Labs constantly challenge this assertion, pointing out that they offer their dogs lives filled with company and comfort. Of course, the same can be said of that caged lion.

Back in the blind at the edge of the marsh, Sonny and I have spent a pleasant hour doing remarkably little. He seriously considered bailing off the bench to chase a muskrat that swam through the middle of the decoy spread, but one hard glance from me was enough to deliver him from temptation. The only birds we've seen overhead were a gathering flock of

blackbirds and a distant pair of hawks. The long Indian summer twilight promises the technical ability to shoot for another half hour, but laws are laws and I rise reluctantly to begin the process of picking up and going home.

Suddenly a dozen blue-wings appear over the tops of the reeds, tearing along in the semi-cohesive relationship to one another only a flock of teal can achieve. I could pretend that legal shooting hours have not yet passed, but they have and I don't. Poised on the bench with legs coiled beneath him like steel springs, Sonny remains waiting for a shot I never take and as the birds flare and claw their way back into the sunset, his disappointment feels palpable. He'll just have to trust me on this one.

And the great thing is, I know he always will.

Labs owners everywhere certainly gain from the fact
that these dogs make valued house pets. But only hunters
understand that Labrador retrievers, purposely-bred over
centuries, achieve their fullest potential and highest happiness
in the fields and marshes in the exhilarating pursuit
of gamebirds. For the sake of Labs everywhere,
it's a secret worth sharing.